MW01264313

THE

Weight

IN

THE

Wait

It's Not the Storm,
It's How You Storm!

ZANETTA L. COLLINS

Trilogy Christian Publishers
A Wholly Owned Subsidiary of Trinity Broadcasting Network
2442 Michelle Drive, Tustin, CA 92780

Copyright © 2020 Zanetta Collins

Scripture quotations marked CEB are from the COMMON ENGLISH BIBLE. © Copyright 2011 COMMON ENGLISH BIBLE. All rights reserved. Used by permission. (www.CommonEnglishBible.com).

Scriptures marked ESV are taken from the THE HOLY BIBLE, ENGLISH STANDARD VERSION: Copyright© 2001 by Crossway, a publishing ministry of Good News Publishers. Used by permission.

Scriptures marked ISV are taken from the INTERNATIONAL STANDARD VERSION (ISV): copyright© 1996-2008 by the ISV Foundation. All rights reserved internationally.

Scripture quotations taken from the 21st Century King James Version®, copyright © 1994. Used by permission of Deuel Enterprises, Inc., Gary, SD 57237. All rights reserved.

Scripture quotations marked MSG are taken from THE MESSAGE, copyright © 1993, 2002, 2018 by Eugene H. Peterson. Used by permission of NavPress. All rights reserved. Represented by Tyndale House Publishers, a Division of Tyndale House Ministries.

All Scripture quotations marked NIV are taken from THE HOLY BIBLE, NEW INTERNATIONAL VERSION®, NIV® Copyright © 1973, 1978, 1984, 2011 by Biblica, Inc.® Used by permission. All rights reserved worldwide.

Scriptures marked NLT are taken from the HOLY BIBLE, NEW LIVING TRANSLATION (NLT): Copyright© 1996, 2004, 2007 by Tyndale House Foundation. Used by permission of Tyndale House Publishers, Inc., Carol Stream, Illinois 60188. All rights reserved. Used by permission.

All rights reserved, including the right to reproduce this book or portions thereof in any form whatsoever. For information, address Trilogy Christian Publishing Rights Department, 2442 Michelle Drive, Tustin, Ca 92780. Trilogy Christian Publishing/ TBN and colophon are trademarks of Trinity Broadcasting Network.

For information about special discounts for bulk purchases, please contact Trilogy Christian Publishing.

Manufactured in the United States of America

Trilogy Disclaimer: The views and content expressed in this book are those of the author and may not necessarily reflect the views and doctrine of Trilogy Christian Publishing or the Trinity Broadcasting Network.

10 9 8 7 6 5 4 3 2 1
Library of Congress Cataloging-in-Publication Data is available.

ISBN 978-1-64773-602-6
E-ISBN 978-1-64773-603-3

Dedication

The Weight in the Wait is dedicated to two words: peace and joy!

At the end of the year 2018, after giving my first fruit for the beginning of the spiritual year (Kairos), the word that God gave me was, "Zanetta, I'm going to give you your joy back!" I had no idea what that meant, but now it's coming together.

Now, in this season, He's removing every weight that so easily beset me!

> Therefore, since we are surrounded by such a huge crowd of witnesses to the life of faith, let us strip off every weight that slows us down, especially the sin that so easily trips us up. And ok let us run with endurance the race God has set before us, because God's removing all of these things from life, I can now have true peace. So, hears to true, joy and peace!

> Hebrews 12:1 (NLT)

About

Zanetta Lee Collins was born to Valerie and Luther Collins, Jr. in Fort Ord, California. At the age of three, her parent's divorce forced her mother to relocate back to her hometown of Cocoa, Florida. Her mother later met and common law married Rudolph Murray, who did his best to provide a stable home. Zanetta's childhood was turbulent and filled with strife. During her early childhood years, Zanetta suffered verbal and physical abuse and was molested by a family member when she was about four or five years old. Her mother was addicted to drugs nearly all of Zanetta's life, from childhood into early adulthood.

All this left a significant void in Zanetta's life. She felt disconnected, alone, and always longed for her mother. Instead of allowing this pain to destroy her, she used this as a catalyst to improve her life. Determined not to follow in her mother's footsteps, she channeled her anger, hurt and frustration into excelling in athletics. Zanetta shined as an athlete and used sports as her gateway to a better education and a brighter future. Upon graduation from high school, Zanetta was awarded an athletic scholarship for basketball. However, during her journey, the residue of her past caused her to suffer from depression, anxiety, and homosexuality.

While striving to obtain a college degree, she encountered additional obstacles and setbacks. She attended four different colleges while trying to find her way and, during the process, she gave birth to a beautiful son, De'Vyon

Collins. Due to sheer determination, after five years, she obtained her BA degree in Psychology from Edward Waters College in Jacksonville, Florida. With degree in hand, it was still difficult to find stable employment to provide for her son.

Shortly after graduation, Zanetta enlisted in the United States Army. This too would present a challenge, as medical issues forced her to be medically discharged. After being back in Cocoa, Florida for several years, the real journey began when she accepted the Lord as her personal Savior on August 18, 2009. This was undoubtedly the best decision she had ever made. It was not until this time that Zanetta began the journey of discovering who she really was and to whom she really belonged.

After giving her life to Christ, she attended cosmetology school and became a licensed cosmetologist. Afterwards, she enrolled at Full Sail University to pursue her Master's degree in Media Design, while establishing her new company ZLC, Incorporated. Unfortunately, with only four classes remaining, Zanetta dropped out of school due to a clerical error at Veterans Affairs which prevented her from receiving financial aid funding.

Within the last five years, Zanetta has published two literary works: *The Colors of My Wings* and *Once Broken*, both of which were published under her own publishing company, The Collins Christian Co. Zanetta's company published *Silence Her No More* for one of her clients, Constance Burrell, and Zanetta works with other authors to create content and their own work.

Forward

While reading this book, I forgot that I was reading a book written by my daughter, Zanetta. The beginning struggles of her journey with Christ were exposed with wisdom and the maturity of freedom. Even when she references current battles, I am able to see and witness her being navigated by her submission to the Holy Spirit. This book is not pretentious, nor does it represent darkness or the trials and tribulations of our lives as insurmountable. It is full of the hope that is found in the Word of God.

What I read was impartation! Those that believe will walk away with a refreshed sense of freedom; those that need to believe will be inspired to do so. In this season, I am sure that God has ordained this vessel and her voice to be a transparent example in a time when identity theft is acceptable, and many are being led astray by the voice of a stranger. Zanetta is boldly proclaiming, "The enemy tries to rob and kill me too, *but* I overcame by the blood of the Lamb, the word of my testimony, and I will not permit my love of this life to lead me to death." This book is a testament to that truth.

It is my esteemed honor to embrace Zanetta as a kingdom daughter. I love you unconditionally.

Forever and Always,

Apostle Shauna Jackson

Table of Contents

Dedication 3

About 5

Forward 7

Acknowledgements 11

Introduction. 13

Court is in Session 15

The Detonator 17

Explosion. 19

Forgiveness Sake 25

Judge Not, Lest You Be Judged 27

From Generation to Generation. 29

Bend, Don't Break. 33

Bridging the Gap 35

The Unconditional 39

Obedience is Greater 45

Blessing of a New Mantel 47

No Giants. 49

Closing Remarks. 57

Acknowledgements

I would like to first give all honor and glory to my Lord and Savior Jesus Christ. You are the Alpha and the Omega, the beginning and the end! In all things you are sovereign.

I would like to thank Sonya Ward of Success Beyond Brilliance. Thanks for putting up with the highs and lows of me!

To my son, no matter what the battle is, I'll always stand in the gap for you because I'm your umbilical cord and God told me a long time ago that everything attached to me wins! I love you to life!

Last, but definitely not least, my Apostle Shauna K. Jackson and my Oil of Joy Family! As always, you guys love me to life… even when I thought I was in my darkest hour, you guys were there! I love you beyond measure!

Introduction

Since I said yes to Christ, I've had small victories, small defeats, big victories and big defeats. At times, I've celebrated in praise and I have wallowed in my own self-pity and sorrow. There were moments when it seemed that I was always miserable, and I could never understand why. Well wait, that's not entirely true. Often, I felt miserable because despite making astronomical changes in my life, I felt as though I didn't see the fruits of my labor and unfortunately, that's where we as a people get it wrong. We go by what we see in the natural versus what God is doing in the spirit.

> So, we fix our eyes not on what is seen,
> but on what is unseen. For what is seen is
> temporary, but what is unseen is eternal.
>
> 2 Corinthians 4:8 (NIV)

I would get upset that my finances were not what I thought they should be; that I was still alone after ten years of waiting and almost nine years celibacy and doing my best to live my life in accordance to His word. I would get upset at the thought of my son, the most important thing in my life, jumping off the deep end into this thing we call life with seemingly no life jacket in sight. It's funny when everyone who is not in your circle looks at you from the outside making judgement based on social media, yet they have no idea what you may be dealing with internally.

One of the hardest things to do as a believer is to praise God in the middle of the storm. It's hard to believe that you're loved when you don't feel it; that you're strong when you feel weak.

> He is before all things, and in Him all
> things hold together!

> Colossians 1:17 (NIV)

All of this happens in the *wait,* and the *weight* is heavy. However, the *goal wait* is near. I heard my Apostle say that in a sermon one Sunday, "the *goal wait* is near." It's near, but first another fight, another battle, another war... the *weight* is heavy, but I still choose to *wait* in God.

What about you? What do you choose? Do you choose to wait in sorrow and pity? Or do you choose to wait in God and in victory? Think about it.

Court is in Session

In my walk with Christ thus far, I had already learned about God being my father and my friend, but now I had to learn about God being my judge. With that being said, it was in the middle of 2018 when my ministry began teaching on the *Courts of Heaven*. One of the main things that I learned from the teaching is that I had the right to go before God with all of my mess; to take it all before the *Courts of Heaven* and ask for justice for those things in my life that were neither right, nor my fault. I also learned that when going before God in the *Courts of Heaven*, I would need to repent beforehand and ask God if there was anything in my life that needed to be uprooted or removed; things that I may have known and others that I may not in reference to my entire bloodline!

Be careful about what you pray for. I had no idea what would come forth during this teaching, but I did it anyway because I needed some things broken off my life, off my son's life, and broken for generations to come. I needed this because while we can't do anything about what happened naturally in the past, we can do something spiritually about all of it—past, present, and future.

So, I went in and I repented. I repented for me, for my son, and for past generations. I asked God to reveal everything in my lineage that I didn't already know if it needed to be uprooted and dealt with! Little did I know, He was going to start with me, but isn't that always the way it goes? He starts with you, the individual, first. Nevertheless, I needed my bloodline cleansed, so, I went before God and prayed:

> "Father God, I come before you right now with a repentant heart on behalf of my father's bloodline, my mother's bloodline, my son, and myself. I am asking you to expose and uproot anything that is not of you, Father God. I pray, Father God, that you break all generational curses in my family and any ungodly soul ties. Father God, I bring my case before you asking you to show me my wrongs and teach me how to make them right. In the name of Jesus, I pray."

The Detonator

I prayed this same prayer for several months and I think around Yom Kippur of 2018, God said, "You need to apologize to one of your cousins," and I said to myself, "*Huh?*"

I wondered which cousin and, more importantly, what did I do? For those of you who don't know, Yom Kippur is known as *The Day of Atonement* or the *Sabbath of Sabbaths*, a twenty-five-hour day for closure and the sealing of our personal *Yearly Book of Life*. It's the day that you are allowed to re-calibrate your life, or a reset if you will. For example, this is the day that you can ask for forgiveness, mend old issues, and close past conflicts!

Not to say that you can't do this any other time during the year, but this specific occasion is the most precise time that the Heavens are open to hear from us! Towards the end of our Apostle's teaching on the *Courts of Heaven*, she expressed a sense of urgency to address anything that needed to be addressed.

So now, back to my cousin that God told me was due an apology. Initially, it threw me for a loop, because this cousin and I had always been tight. Both of our mothers had battled drug addiction for most of our lives, and that experience created a tight knit bond between us despite our age gap. Needless to say, I was lost as to what I had done! As I continued to pray about it, the Holy Spirit dropped the first bomb on me.

He took me back to when I was in my early twenties and my cousin was still this shy and chubby, yet adorable, teen. I think he was about sixteen years old at the time, and I remembered he loved to hang out with me and my friends. One day, a couple of my friends and I were hanging out. They thought my cousin was so adorable, yet he lacked the confidence that we all had at his age, and so, a proposition was presented to break him out of his shell.

While I was in the living room, a friend joined my cousin in one of the back rooms of the house. At the time, I thought nothing of it because I was taught that certain things that took place between a younger man and an older woman were considered rites of passage. I don't really know what happened behind that closed door, if anything at all, but God reminded me that I could've possibly perpetuated a cycle.

With this new-found revelation and my being a new creature in Christ, I had to go back to this now-grown man and ask for his forgiveness for something that I thought was okay due to my upbringing. My cousin really didn't think much of it, but I had to make it right with him and, most importantly, right before God.

Explosion

After apologizing to my little cousin about my conduct, I felt so much better. Four months of 2019 had passed before I made it through that test, and it was now Passover. Passover, which is also known as "Pesach" in Hebrew, is the Jewish festival commemorating the liberation of the children of Israel, who were led out of Egypt and slavery by Moses. Passover also represents God's "passing over" the Jewish homes during the tenth plague of Egypt where God slayed all first-born Egyptian children. Before the plague began, the Israelites were instructed to smear the blood of a lamb over their doors so that the plague wouldn't kill their first born.

During that week, my Apostle said to me several times, "Zanetta, I really believe that this is your last leg of deliverance." She also said, "There is a hidden level of perversion that needs to be exposed and eradicated for you to walk into complete freedom."

Now, I'm thinking, "*Dang, what could that be?*" I said to myself, "*I'm not doing anything.*" So I asked her, "What could it be? I'm not doing anything."

My Apostle replied, "Zanetta, I don't know, but I believe God will show you in time."

Her response upset me, because it made me question what else I could possibly do. I felt like I'd become the closest one could be to a nun at that time. I asked what else needed to be done, but her response remained the same, "I don't know. It's something hidden deep down inside and God's going to have to reveal it to you."

Boy, did He ever reveal it to me! It was bad enough that I put my little cousin in a situation that was basically a form of molestation. Now, one of the most horrific things I could ever imagine or confess was staring me directly in my face like a raging pit bull ready to devour me. I have never been fearful of being open about anything that I've endured before or during my walk with Christ, but this... *this* scared me!

While sitting at my apostle's house, discussing everything happening with my son, my apostle's daughter and I began having a side conversation about a young lady I used to date back in the day. This young lady and I actually dated off and on for about four years, and my apostle's daughter asked how old this young lady and I were when we dated. Of course, in trying to answer that question, I sat there and began counting backwards, but both parties were side-tracked, and our conversation ended before I could answer.

When I got home, the Holy Spirit spoke to me and asked, "Zanetta, how old were you when you dated her?"

Then came that Mack truck, the C4 powerful enough to level buildings, the explosion of all explosions. Right then and there, the Holy Spirit said, "Zanetta, you were an adult, and the young lady that you were dating at the time was *not*." The realization that she was a young girl and not an adult hit me, and I just broke down and hit the floor! I thought, "*Oh my god, what have I done? What have I done?*" I was sick to my stomach. I was crying and shaking. I was seeing myself in the same light as those people who had molested children or sexually abused a teen.

In my mind's eye, I saw and condemned myself the same way I had seen and condemned those predators, and now I was disgusted with myself.

All these years I wanted to protect my son from those people, but immediately I started to think my son should've been protected from me. While I have never done anything—and I mean *nothing*—to my son or anyone else for that matter, those thoughts raced through my head! The *weight* of guilt weighed on me so much so, that I felt like I was the one from whom people needed to protect their kids. Although I would never do such a thing, that's how I felt in that moment. The fact that I defiled this young lady truly breaks my heart, and the crazy thing was, I knew she was younger than me. At the time, I felt it was okay because I had permission to date her. Her mom had given me the green light to date her.

I guess somewhere in all that, at that stage in my life, I deemed it okay because I had permission to date her. This experience goes to show that even when you are given permission or presented with a piece of the truth, and the enemy can use partial truths to set you up for failure.

> "I have the right to do anything," you say—
> but not everything is beneficial. "I have the
> right to do anything"—but not everything
> is constructive."
>
> 1 Corinthians 10:23 (NIV)

Somehow, in my head, I felt her mother's permission made it okay. It just goes to show you how truly messed up you are when you are deep in sin. Now, God is showing me it wasn't okay! Had I been right, I wouldn't have been so devasted and disgusted with myself!

After a few days of playing everything over in my

head, God said, "You have to call her. You have to call her and get this right with her." Now, this young lady and I hadn't talked in quite some time, mainly because our relationship had always had its ups and downs. We fought, we argued, we made up... that was our cycle. Even after coming to Christ, for some reason, I still always had this attachment to her, but I knew it wasn't a *soul tie*. A soul tie is defined as a spiritual connection between two people who have been physically intimate with each other or who have had an intense emotional or spiritual association or relationship. Until this revelation, I never understood the true definition of a soul tie.

So again, after getting myself together and mustering up enough strength to call her, I dialed her number and told her that I really needed to talk to her about us. She was open to having a conversation, but before I could explain myself, I broke down again when the realization of what I had done to her hit me all over again. She said, "Netta," she has always called me Netta, "What's wrong? Just say it!"

I started, "God showed me that when we were together, I was wrong because of the age difference."

As I was releasing all the things God showed me, she stopped me and asked, "Zanetta, why do you think we met? Why do you think we ended up in each other's lives?"

I was so emotional that I couldn't really think straight in the moment, so I responded, "I don't know."

I continued talking and apologizing and, in doing so, God answered the question for me. He said, "You came into her life for just this reason. This very moment is going to change her life and begin a shift in her to turn back to me!" I was amazed!

At the end of the conversation, she said, "Zanetta, you don't owe me an apology, because I did what I wanted to do, but if you need it, I forgive you," and I broke down again!

Afterwards, the conversation, the situation, it all just kept playing in my head over and over again. God showed me that despite all of our mess, the reason we had truly met all those years ago, was for this very moment in time; an opportunity to show her a believer that was truly humble, sincere, and vulnerable! She got to see a believer that was yielded, and I truly believe the seed to start her back on her path towards a true and living God and begin her walk with Christ was planted on that day.

Then God said, "Now, you get to see what real forgiveness looks like! *Now* you can sincerely forgive your uncle who molested you!"

"If you forgive those who sin against you,
your heavenly Father will forgive you. But
if you refuse to forgive others, your Father
will not forgive your sins.

Matthew 6:14-15 (ESV)

Forgiveness Sake

I find it funny that we as people are always so quick to judge, but when God reveals our true self, all you can do is drop to your knees and ask for forgiveness!

Forgiveness is the *process* of forgiving or being forgiven. Also known as clemency, lenience, tolerance, or pardon, it is the process of releasing anger or resentment towards others for an offense. Forgiveness is a two-way street. I say that because we all want to be forgiven, but when it's time to forgive, most times, we can't.

Oftentimes, we forgive in part, not totality, and that's not of God. God requires us to forgive in totality so we can get the fullness of His blessing for our lives! He can't do that if we don't do our part!

First, God had to show me myself and that I wasn't perfect. Once He showed me my true self, I had to make corrections. Most of us can't do that because of our pride, however, that will kill you, and the future that God has for you! After going back and apologizing, God said, "*Now* you can forgive your uncle!" Don't you get it? God had to first show me how to tear down my walls and pre-conceptions to get me to a place where He knew I could acknowledge my being fallible!

It's not that I didn't know that I was capable of making mistakes. I knew this, but in learning true humility, I was moved to know this on another level. These experiences were teaching me to bow before God so that I could stand before any man. Despite all my flaws and faults, I learned that as long as I have the right mindset and a clean heart, God can still use me! That is what these tests were teaching me and now that I understand that, I can embrace it.

Judge Not, Lest You Be Judged

In addition to teaching me humility, God taught me about judgement and being judgmental. I'm not talking about *righteous judgement*, because we do have the right for righteous judgement. I'm talking about the pre-judgement of people and situations.

Again, not that I didn't know about being judgmental because, let's not forget, I was once the "gay girl," so I know all too well about judgement! I got the rolling eyes, the side conversations, and of course the staring. People looked at me like I was a unicorn, so I really did my best to make sure that I wasn't judgmental!

God's word states:

> "Do not judge, and you will not be judged. Do not condemn, and you will not be condemned. Forgive, and you will be forgiven. Give, and it will be given to you. A good measure, pressed down, shaken together, and running over, will be poured into your lap. For with the measure you use, it will be measured to you." He also told them this parable: "Can the blind lead the blind? Will they not both fall into a pit? The student is not above the teacher, but everyone who is fully trained will be

like their teacher. Why do you look at the
speck of sawdust in your brother's eye and
pay no attention to the plank in your own
eye? How can you say to your brother,
'Brother, let me take the speck out of your
eye,' when you yourself fail to see the plank
in your own eye? You hypocrite first take
the plank out of your eye, and then you
will see clearly to remove the speck from
your brother's eye.'"

Luke 6:37-42 (NIV)

When you judge another person without probable
cause or in a hypocritical way, you pay the price. It steals
other people's hope and joy and makes it impossible for
others to trust God's power. Judgment aids in planting
seeds of unforgiveness and cultivates pride. All of this
pollutes the heart and magnifies our own sins in God's
eyes.

Do not judge others, and you will not
be judged. For you will be treated as you
treat others. The standard you used in
judging is the standard by which you will
be judged.

Matthew 7:1-2 (NLT)

ZANETTA L. COLLINS

From Generation to Generation

I believe that because God exposed this issue in my life/ generation, I was able to expose it in the generation before me with my uncle. I also remember someone else in the generation before me discussing an issue with the previous generation before my uncle. Can you see the pattern that had presented itself after my going into the *Courts of Heaven* and praying for everything to be exposed and uprooted? God exposed *generational curses*. A generational curse is a defilement that has been passed down from one generation to another. For examples, see topics discussed in chapters three and four.

> Keeping mercy for thousands, forgiving
> iniquity and transgression and sin, and
> that will by no means clear the guilty;
> visiting (punishing) the iniquity of the
> fathers upon the children, and upon the
> children's children, unto the third and to
> the fourth generation.
>
> Exodus 34:7 (KJ21)

Honestly, there's no doubt in my mind that the issue of molestation goes back further than just those three generations.

I also believe unforgiveness is a great way to open the door for "generational curses" (i.e. I had unforgiveness and bitterness in my heart and in that I gave legal grounds for the enemy to live in me).

> Let everyone be subject to the governing
> authorities, for there is no authority
> except that which God has established. The
> authorities that exist have been established
> by God. Consequently, whoever rebels
> against the authority is rebelling against
> what God has instituted, and those who
> do so will bring judgment on themselves.
> For rulers hold no terror for those who
> do right, but for those who do wrong. Do
> you want to be free from fear of the one
> in authority? Then do what is right and
> you will be commended. For the one in
> authority is God's servant for your good.
> But if you do wrong, be afraid, for rulers
> do not bear the sword for no reason. They
> are God's servants, agents of wrath to bring
> punishment on the wrongdoer. Therefore,
> it is necessary to submit to the authorities,
> not only because of possible punishment
> but also as a matter of conscience. This
> is also why you pay taxes, for the authori-
> ties are God's servants, who give their full
> time to governing. Give to everyone what
> you owe them: If you owe taxes, pay taxes;

if revenue, then revenue; if respect, then
respect; if honor, then honor.

Romans 13: 1-7 (NIV)

In holding unforgiveness and bitterness in my heart,
I opened myself up to generational curses, unbeknownst
to me! The good news is that the Blood of Jesus is more
powerful than any bondage that may have been handed
down to you! You can be completely released from the
effects of any generational curses handed down to you
simply by repenting.

Not condoning any forms of perversion allows us
to see things through other people's eyes and gain a
different perspective. You know that old saying, "Don't
say anything to me until you have walked a mile in my
shoes"? It's not biblical, but it works!

It's very hard to stand in front of people and address
issues that you have never endured. Even if God provides
revelation in these areas, it is still very hard to go before
man if you have never walked in whatever issue or sin
that's been placed before you.

Bend, Don't Break

How many of you know that when God starts pouring revelation into you, the enemy increases the distractions and issues of life? Well, if you didn't know, now you know. As if everything that I'd been through up until this point was enough, that's exactly what happened to me!

After my son turned eighteen, with only one year of high school remaining and he feeling as if he were grown, he decided to run away. Initially, I was mad! I wanted to lash out at him and the people he was dealing with. My reacting in anger showed me that I hadn't let go of an old piece of myself, "the fighter." I kept trying to hold onto that piece of myself because I thought it would make me seem weak, and I couldn't have that. Then God said, "Zanetta, that's pride."

Pride is an inordinate self-esteem; an unreasonable feeling of superiority as to one's talents, beauty, wealth, rank, and so forth; disdainful behavior or treatment; insolence or arrogance of demeanor; haughty bearing.

I was like, "God, what am I just supposed to do? Am I supposed to let this dude punk me and disrespect me along with the people he's running around with?" Clearly, they didn't know me, so they needed to know *me*!

I wanted to just go over to the house where he was living, locked and loaded, but God said, "No! This angry person is no longer you, and you don't have to choose that path. Zanetta, you can't violate the God in you nor resurrect the old you."

I knew God was right, but inside I wanted to fight

because that's what I knew! I *knew* how to fight and how to shut you out once I was tired of being tired or hurt. I learned that from never having a relationship with my birth father and my mother being high or nowhere to be found. One of my coping mechanisms was shutting down so I wouldn't get hurt by or be disappointed with the people I loved. The other, was anger/fighting. That's how I protected myself.

Even as an adult in my relationships, I loved hard. I gave my all until others hurt me. Once hurt, part of me would keep trying, but in the back of my mind, I had already begun erasing you from my life. I continued on this way until I was faced with my son running away. The one person that I loved more than life itself disappointed and hurt me to my core! It's like he made the world think that I was this horrible parent, as if I had him tied up in the basement and tortured him!

After he ran away, I was faced with looking him in his face and treating him like everything was okay and, honestly, I didn't know how to do that. I wanted to shut down and turn my back on him just as he had turned his back on me.

I actually attempted it, but God said, "Zanetta, that's not you anymore." As much as I wanted to turn my back on my son, I couldn't, no matter what he had done or what he was doing. It wasn't in me anymore to be so quick to walk away like I had in the past. In this moment, God said, "That's not unconditional love. Zanetta, I need you to learn unconditional love because that's the love that I need you to have for your son and my people." I could no longer magnify the circumstances because getting up and making things right on my end was greater than me dying!

Bridging the Gap

Yes, coming to Christ was hard. One of the hardest tasks that I've had in Christ is to allow Him to be my EVERY-THING...to be my mother, my father, my teacher, my healer, my lover, my friend...my EVERYTHING! I was okay with all of those except father and lover! For the longest time, the thought of those two together have always rubbed me the wrong way because I was molested by a family member and the thought of that turns my stomach. Before you ask, no, my father wasn't the one who molested me, but I was molested by a family member that should have been protecting me. I just couldn't wrap my head around the father/lover concept. I understood it in the natural, but I just couldn't mesh the two together. I had no vantage point to gain revelation about God being my father and my lover.

I struggled with Him being my father mainly because I really never had a healthy example of what a father/daughter relationship was supposed to look like. My real father and I talked *once* when he threatened to take my life. I saw him three times around the age of eight, again at the age of forty. And lastly, the week before my forty-first birthday, while he was on his death bed when my sister and I had to decide whether to pull the plug. My stepfather, on the other hand, was actually a great man and a great provider, but nothing more! He never told me he was proud of me or that he loved me, and I needed that. So, my struggles with that perpetuated my allowing external female/male relationships to be my outlet.

What I did know of an ideal father figure was that he's supposed to be the provider, the protector, and the head of the home. So, in my relationship with God, even though it was a struggle relinquishing authority, I could at least get with those aspects of a father/daughter relationship. Over time, I was able to submit to His authority as "Abba Father," but now, I'm being faced with what I would call one of the most necessary and profound tests in my relationship with "Abba Father."

If God is my everything or should be my everything, how do I get to that final piece? How do I bridge the gap between God being my *father* and God being my *lover*? Coming from a place of being molested as a kid, this notion turned my stomach upside down. I had no clue how to merge that final piece of the puzzle. Because my eyes are beginning to open and revelation is seeming to be pouring in like a flood, this ate me up inside; I had no clue how to settle into that internal place, and that tore me to shreds!

All my life, even though I can naturally understand that intimacy is deeper than sex, when it truly came down to it, I had always equated intimacy to sex; using people or things bridge the gap between the two to fill a void. I realized that I had to stop looking for and expecting for someone else or something in the natural to fill the void in me.

This realization upsets me because I've been saved going on ten years now, but even after ten years of serving God, I'm still looking around for someone or something to fill that black hole inside. All I could hear is God saying, "Zanetta, you don't have to look any further. I'm right here, right where I've always been."

However, I couldn't reach Him because I didn't know

how to let go and let God love me and through every-thing and every situation. That... *that* is something that I desperately wanted and needed in this season especially because I know I don't want to get married and bring these issues into my marriage. We as a people tend to get married and end up alone in a marriage or alone in love because we never fill that gaping hole inside. We look to our spouse or others to fill a void that will never be filled by an external force. It just doesn't work that way. God wants to fill those voids and truthfully, He's the only one that can if, and only if, you let Him!

The Unconditional

Man, coming out of homosexuality was extremely difficult! It was probably the worst stronghold I had ever dealt with. Somehow, this fight, this war, was different. This war was not for me or anyone else, but my son—my boy, my heartbeat, the reason that I breathe.

So, I went in, and I began to pray:

> "Father God, I need you now like never before! Father God, I bind, prohibit, and disallow everything that's coming against my son and my family right now. I pray, Father God, that you uproot anything that is not of you, God! I pray, Father God, that you guard his ear gates and his eye gates! And I pray that his heart isn't hardened by the things of this world. In Jesus's name, I pray!"

Now, my son is my new battle, he's my new war; I need God more than ever!

My heart is weak, and my body is heavy, as if there's a thorn in my side like:

> Even though I have received such wonderful revelations from God. So, to keep me from becoming proud, I was given a thorn in my flesh, a messenger from Satan to torment me and keep me from

becoming proud. Three different times
I begged the Lord to take it away. Each
time he said, "My grace is all you need. My
power works best in weakness." So now I
am glad to boast about my weaknesses, so
that the power of Christ can work through
me.

2 Corinthians 12:7-9 (NLT)

Or like:

Then Jesus said to his disciples, "If any of
you wants to be my follower, you must give
up your own way, take up your cross, and
follow me. If you try to hang on to your
life, you will lose it. But if you give up your
life for my sake, you will save it. And what
do you benefit if you gain the whole world
but lose your own soul? Is anything worth
more than your soul?"

Matthew 16:24-26 (NLT)

This cross that I was created to bear is sitting heavy.
The *weight* in the *wait* seems as if it's about to break me! I
could say the same thing in reference to when I first came
to Christ, but this *weight* was different. I would look over
and if I didn't see my son, my heart would skip a beat! It
was like my air was stifled because in the natural I didn't
know if he was ok!

That's how the enemy works! The enemy knew that he
really only had one more shot to get me; one more shot

ZANETTA L. COLLINS

that could possibly derail my path, and that was to use my son! Yet and still, all I continued to hear was, "Zanetta, you have to let go and trust."

You know, we as believers say we trust God until we are confronted with the hard things. We don't know how to let go, and that feeling of fear begins to creep in. For me, my fear of failing as a mother and not being able to face God's people is creeping in, and, if I'm being honest, I've felt this way before. I've questioned how I am to serve God's people if I couldn't stand on His word. I said yes to God and chose to serve Him. If I couldn't stand after choosing to walk away from homosexuality, and I can't stand now when my son has seemingly walked away from God's arms and his family, his blood, how do I continue to hold on to God when what I see doesn't add up to the life I want to live? God told me of the life that would be mine if I chose to serve Him, but the *weight* is stifling!

Remember earlier, when I told you how I tend to shut down when I'm not being treated right? At one point, after being gone and not speaking to me, my son asked for a haircut. Originally, I laughed and said no. Then, I said yes, because I was trying to fight through my anger and pain. Ultimately, I wanted to first be right with God. So reluctantly, I said yes, he came over, and while cutting his hair, I decided to use the moment to attempt a civilized conversation. We had a small talk, and I asked him if he was coming home, but he said no. This enraged me!

When I got finished cutting his hair, I told him, "Since you want to be grown, grown people pay all of their own bills, period!" I told him from that point on haircuts were twenty-five dollars every time he sat in my chair!

As my son got up to give me a hug, I began shutting down and preparing for the worst, both emotionally and in the natural. I gave him a sideways hug as if he were a stranger to me, and God said, "Zanetta, that's not love, but I will teach you the true meaning of unconditional love!" Of course, I wouldn't really turn away from my son. I was hurt, and I wanted him to feel the way he made me feel, but De'Vyon could not have cared less in that moment. He was going to do what he wanted!

So again, God said, "I'm going to teach you how to love! How to love when it hurts and there's no end to your pain in sight!"

In case you didn't know, there are four types of love in the Bible: Eros, Storge, Philia, and Agape. *Eros*, a Greek word for sensual or romantic, refers to sexual love. *Storge* love is familial, like the affectionate bonds that develop naturally between parents and their children, siblings, etc. *Philia*, the most general type of love, is the intimate love in the Bible practiced among Christians; it describes the power of true friendship. Finally, there's *Agape*, the highest form of the four types of love in the Bible. Agape defines God's immeasurable, incomparable love for all! It is perfect, unconditional, sacrificial, and pure like the divine love that comes from God.

Clearly, I've experienced Eros, Storge, and Philia but now God wanted me to reach the phase of *Agape*; the *unconditional* love with my son. So, I had to figure out how to get there. It was so hard for me, but I'm a true believer in sparing the rod and spoiling the child:

> Whoever spares the rod hates their
> children, but the one who loves their
> children is careful to discipline them.

Proverbs 13:24 (NIV)

Through it all, the one thing I could hold on to was God's word. I knew that God said:

> Then Peter came to him and asked, "Lord, how often should I forgive someone who sins against me? Seven times?"
>
> "No, not seven times," Jesus replied, "but seventy times seven!
>
> Matthew 18:21-22 (NLT)

Boom! In that moment, it hit me. God was telling me that no matter what my son does, I've been charged with forgiving. God said:

> "No matter how much pain he causes you, you are charged with forgiving him. No matter how many times he disrespects you, you are charged with forgiving him. No matter how many tears you cry you are still charged with forgiving him 70 x 7, bottom line!"

Truth be told, as bad as the situation seems, God has stayed the hand of the enemy on my son's behalf and mine.

> No temptation has overtaken you except what is common to mankind. And God is faithful; he will not let you be tempted beyond what you can bear. But when you

are tempted, he will also provide a way out
so that you can endure it.

1 Corinthians 10:13 (NIV)

It's even more important that none of us think more highly of ourselves than we should!

Because of the privilege and authority
God has given me, I give each of you this
warning: Don't think you are better than
you really are. Be honest in your evalua-
tion of yourselves, measuring yourselves by
the faith God has given us.

Romans 12:3 (NLT)

Truth is, we all have faults, we all have shortcomings, we all have fallen short of the glory of God!

For everyone has sinned; we all fall short
of God's glorious standard

Romans 3:23 (NLT)

No one is perfect! So now, no matter what my son does, I pray for him and I forgive him! Is it hard? Yes. Do I want to give up? Yes. However, I can't give up because my life, his life, and your life depend on me never giving up and always holding on to my faith!

Obedience is Greater

As I've stated so many different times on many different occasions while writing this book, there are plenty of things that are hard to do once you come to Christ. Truthfully, no matter where life takes you, you'll have hard times and you'll have easy times; what we Christians typically call peaks and valleys. You can either go through the hard times with or without Christ. Trust me, going through *with* Christ makes it all a little easier! Christ serves as a GPS saying, "Don't go that way. There's danger. Go *this* way because there's a blessing waiting for you." I never would have gotten to that place without choosing to be obedient to God's will and way for my life.

> But Samuel replied, "What is more
> pleasing to the LORD: your burnt
> offerings and sacrifices or your obedience
> to his voice? Listen! Obedience is better
> than sacrifice, and submission is better
> than offering the fat of rams.
>
> 1 Samuel 15:22 (NLT)

As much as I despise some of the revelations that God revealed to me during this season of my life, I'm also very grateful. It was only in my obedience to serving a true and living God, that I can now take the information that He's given me like a right hook on the jaw and keep it pushing.

That's His will for my life! As much as I want to cower away and never discuss this ever again in life, He taught me how to expose and deal with so many issues that lurk in the shadows of our minds, relationships, homes, and most importantly, our spirits!

God reminded me that none of us are exempt from dealing with sin! Before, there was no way on God's green earth anyone could have ever confronted me with my past! I would have denied it all until the day I died because it disgusts me. In my right mind, I would've never done that to someone else after it was done to me, but that's sin for you!

It was no different than having a druggie for a mother who never realized she not only stole material possessions from you as a child, but that she also literally stole your childhood from you! It's no different than your father robbing you of what to look for in a man because he was never around to serve as the blueprint for the type of man you needed! It's no different than dating a younger person, even with "permission," instead of being their light in a dark place! None of it is right because it's all sin, and only in obedience can such things be completely revealed to you!

Blessing of a New Mantel

Throughout the years since I've said yes to Christ, God has chastised me and beat my behind! On the flip side, He has also protected me and held me tight when I had no one to tell me that everything was going to be okay.

> God "will repay each person according
> to what they have done." To those
> who by persistence in doing good seek
> glory, honor, and immortality, he will
> give eternal life. But for those who are
> self-seeking and who reject the truth and
> follow evil, there will be wrath and anger.
>
> Romans 2:6-8 (NIV)

In all of this, the biggest reward is the fact that I obeyed! When I was wounded, I obeyed. When I was broken, I obeyed. When my mind was warped, I obeyed. God said:

> "Because of your obedience, I was able to
> take a potentially volatile situation and
> use it for the betterment of my kingdom.
> Because you obeyed, I was able to open
> you up to more revelation. Because of your
> obedience, you were open to understand-
> ing unconditional love and forgiveness.
> Because you obeyed, as long as you don't

harshly judge my people, you now have a better chance that I won't harshly judge you. Because of your obedience, generational curses are now broken off your life and your lineage. Because you obeyed me, your son is covered! Now, you may really understand that *obedience* is far greater than sacrifice. *Now*, I can bless you; Not that I hadn't blessed you before, but now it's time to bless you beyond measure! It's time for man to look upon you, Zanetta, and know that many are called, but few are chosen, and I have chosen *you* to spread my gospel."

God said to me, "Welcome to your *Goal Wait*, new mantel!"

No Giants

In the beginning of 2019, I received a word from God and the word was, "This year you will get your joy back!"

You are probably saying, "Okay, when is this supposed to happen; because it seems like she's having a lot of issues?" But that's because you are looking through your natural eyes. With your natural eyes, you see issues, you see problems, you see chaos!

But God said, "I call you daughter, and I have have given you everything you need; it's all inside of you!" He said, "Stand up and plant your feet firm on the foundation that you have worked so hard to build in me!" He said, "Every mountain that has stood, Zanetta, tell it to move!"

> I tell you the truth, you can say to this mountain, 'May you be lifted up and thrown into the sea,' and it will happen. But you must really believe it will happen and have no doubt in your heart. I tell you, you can pray for anything, and if you believe that you've received it, it will be yours.
>
> Mark 11:23-24 (NLT)

There are many stories in the Bible about fighting the righteous fight and overcoming adversities or overcoming the enemy. I can give you three examples off the top of my head.

The first one is the story of the Walls of Jericho. In this story, Joshua and the Israelites arrived at the land that God had promised them. Even though the city was well fortified, Joshua followed the instructions that God had given him to over-take the city of Jericho.

> "You and your fighting men should march around the town once a day for six days. Seven priests will walk ahead of the Ark, each carrying a ram's horn. On the seventh day you are to march around the town seven times, with the priests blowing the horns. When you hear the priests give one long blast on the rams' horns, have all the people shout as loud as they can. Then the walls of the town will collapse, and the people can charge straight into the town."

> Joshua 6:3-5 (NLT)

That's exactly what happened!

Because of Joshua's obedience, Joshua was able to hear the instructions of God and carry out the plan to over-take the enemy and walk in the fullness of what God had for Joshua and the Israelites.

The second one is the story of David and Goliath. This story is about the Philistines and the Israelites going to war. The Philistines had this champion giant fighter named Goliath who stood over six cubits. And then there was David. David was the youngest of four sons; while the older three fought in combat, David went back and forth from Saul to tend to his father sheep in Bethlehem. So, one day, David was basically instructed to take provisions to his older brothers and the commanders that were fighting. While David was delivering the provisions, he heard Goliath shouting as he always did; but he also noticed that every time Goliath did this, the Israelites ran because they were afraid! David then asked, "What would be done for the man who kills Goliath?"

The response was basically whoever kills Goliath will have great wealth, his family will never have to pay taxes, and he will be given Saul's daughter for marriage. To make a long story short, Saul sent David his servant to face Goliath. Saul dressed David in his own tunic and gave him armor and a bronze helmet; as David fastened the sword and tried to walk around in it, he said, "I'm not used to this! I can't use this." So, he took it all off. Then he took his staff, five smooth stones, and what we in today's world would call a sling shot and approached the Philistine giant Goliath.

Goliath took one look at David and thought, *"This is just a boy."*

David said, "All those gathered here will know that it is not by sword or spear that the Lord saves; for the battle is the Lord's, and He will give all of you into our hands." As the battle incited, David quickly ran to meet Goliath. He reached into his sack and took out a stone; he slung it, and it hit Goliath on his forehead. The stone then sank into the Philistine's forehead, and the giant fell face down on the ground!

David didn't need a sword; he took five smooth stones of which he only used one because he stood on the Word of God. He didn't need a shield because he was covered under the blood of Jesus, he was covered by God's grace and God's unfailing hand which protected him!

This last story took place before Jesus was even born. In the book of Daniel, there is a story about three young men who held onto their belief in God, even when threatened with a fiery death. These three young Hebrew boys—Hananiah, Mishael, and Azariah—were taken and held captive in Babylon along with other prominent Israelites. There was also a fourth young man by the name of Daniel. Once in captivity, the youths were given new names. Daniel was now called Belteshazzar; Hananiah was called Shadrach; Mishael was called Meshach; and Azariah was called Abednego.

These four Hebrew youths soon proved to be very wise. As a result, they found favor with King Nebuchadnezzar. When Daniel turned out to be the only man capable of interpreting one of Nebuchadnezzar's troubling dreams, the king placed him in a high position over the whole province of Babylon, including over all the wise men of the land. At Daniel's request, the king appointed Shadrach, Meshach, and Abednego as Daniel's advisors.

King Nebuchadnezzar had this huge golden statue built as a symbol of his power. He then commanded that everyone bow down and worship this image whenever they heard the sound of his musical herald. Those who disobeyed would be thrown into a blazing furnace.

Shadrach, Meshach, and Abednego, however, worshipped only the true and living God and they refused to bow down to the false idol. They were then brought before Nebuchadnezzar to face their fate but remained steadfast and unmovable in the face of the king's demand to bow down before the golden statue. They said:

"O Nebuchadnezzar, we have no need to

answer you in this matter. If this be so,
our God whom we serve is able to deliver
us from the burning fiery furnace, and he
will deliver us out of your hand, O king.
But if not, be it known to you, O king, that
we will not serve your gods or worship the
golden image that you have set up."

Daniel 3:16-18 (MSG)

Furious, Nebuchadnezzar ordered the furnace to be heated seven times hotter than average. Shadrach, Meshach, and Abednego were bound and cast into the flames. But as King Nebuchadnezzar looked into the furnace, he was amazed at what he saw:

"But I see four men unbound, walking in
the midst of the fire, and they are not hurt;
and the appearance of the fourth is like a
son of the gods."

Daniel 3:25 (ESV)

Then the king called the men to come out of the furnace. Shadrach, Meshach, and Abednego emerged unharmed, with not even a hair on their heads singed or the smell of smoke on their clothing. Needless to say, this made quite an impression on Nebuchadnezzar, who declared:

"Blessed be the God of Shadrach,
Meshach, and Abednego, who has sent

His angel and delivered His servants, who trusted in Him, and set aside the king's command, and yielded up their bodies rather than serve and worship any god except their own God."

Daniel 3:28 (ESV)

Through God's miraculous deliverance of Shadrach, Meshach, and Abednego that day, Nebuchadnezzar declared that the remaining Israelites in captivity were now protected from harm and were guaranteed freedom of worship. And Shadrach, Meshach, and Abednego received a royal promotion.

In all three of these stories, several things happened. In each story, there was a giant of some sort. In every story, there was a person or people that were considered less than. But, the people listed above all served a true and living God; they all stood on their faith and the Word of God. Every single one of them stood on their faith and destroyed giants!

Finally, be strong in the Lord and in his mighty power. Put on the full armor of God, so that you can take your stand against the devil's schemes. For our struggle is not against flesh and blood, but against the rulers, against the authorities, against the powers of this dark world and against the spiritual forces of evil in the heavenly realms. Therefore, put on the full armor of God, so that when the day of evil comes, you may be able to stand your ground, and after you have done everything, to stand. Stand firm then, with the belt of truth buckled around your waist, with the breastplate of righteousness in place, and with your feet fitted with the readiness that comes from the gospel of peace. In addition to all this, take up the shield of faith, with which you can extinguish all the flaming arrows of the evil one. Take the helmet of salvation and the sword of the Spirit, which is the word of God. And pray in the Spirit on all occasions with all kinds of prayers and requests. With this in mind, be alert and always keep on praying for all the Lord's people.

Ephesians 6:10-18 (NIV)

Closing Remarks

The funny thing about this particular book: when I first started writing it, the closing remarks were one of the first things I wrote. I am pretty sure that this was my way of showing God that in spite of what I was seeing around me, I trusted Him; that somewhere inside, despite what I was seeing, I knew He had the final say. Honestly, that is what God wants for us. He wants us to praise Him in advance for the victories to come.

I had three phrases, the closing remarks, the empty pages in between, and a mindset that was struggling! I had blind eyes, a hardening heart, closed ears, and weak knees. Oh, and one more thing I had was a mustard seed of faith!

> "You don't have enough faith," Jesus told them. I tell you the truth, if you had faith even as small as a mustard seed, you could say to this mountain, "Move from here to there," and it would move. Nothing would be impossible."
>
> Matthew 17:20 (NLT)

That's all I needed! That covered all the previously stated issues. Faith was all He wanted, and I knew that somewhere inside of me, between the blank pages, my victory was at hand. My victory would not be reached by my hand, but by God's hands and His hand alone. God uses our impossible circumstances so that He can get the glory and shine His light!

> All this is for your benefit, so that the grace that is reaching more and more people may cause thanksgiving to overflow to the glory of God.

> Corinthians 4:15 (NIV)

I'm the type of person that strives to do things the right way. In this season, I've been faced with so many tests and so much revelation, but through it all, I've shifted into a deeper intimacy with Him.

God has been building me all these years, and now, who I really am is beginning to take shape. I had to get to the point that I didn't need validation from woman, man, or any other external source. I had to trust the process!

> Jeremiah received the Lord's word: Go down to the potter's house, and I'll give you instructions about what to do there. So, I went down to the potter's house; he was working on the potter's wheel. But the piece he was making was flawed while still in his hands, so the potter started on another, as seemed best to him. Then the Lord's word came to me: House of Israel, can't I deal with you like this potter, declares the Lord? Like clay in the potter's hand, so are you in mine, house of Israel! At any time, I may announce that I will

dig up, pull down, and destroy a nation or kingdom; but if that nation I warned turns from its evil, then I'll relent and not carry out the harm I intended for it. At the same time, I may announce that I will build and plant a nation or kingdom.

Jeremiah 18:1-9 (CEB)

and

But now, Lord, you are our father. We are the clay, and You are our potter. All of us are the work of Your hand.

Isaiah 64:8 (ISV)

A lot of times, God allows us to be in uncomfortable situations because in that place of discomfort sometimes miracles are birthed. When we are comfortable, we tend to grow complacent, meaning we become overly content. While in that uncomfortable place, this is where God tends to perfect our worship. In the uncomfortable place, you become rooted and assured of who God has called you to be and this strengthens faith!

The enemy has tried time and time again to drag me back to who I used to be, but I am determined to make it to the other side. God has given me rest from my enemies.

At this point, the only way that these things have any access to me is if I keep inviting old mindsets back in. The enemy wanted me to believe that all the work that I've done was temporary, but the truth is, I am married to the King of kings and the Lord of lords. Our marriage is for eternity, and it can only be given away, not taken!

I had to realize that it was ok to recognize my crown. I have made it through to the other side and I will never be that person again. No matter what is going on around me, I can't, and I won't!

Recently, I had a vision of me walking in a valley with a sword in my hand surrounded by lions. This vision proved to me that I'm in a new place. I'm walking into a new season of authority and I'm walking into it boldly!

No more *Weight in the Wait!*

CPSIA information can be obtained
at www.ICGtesting.com
Printed in the USA
BVHW041141030422
633065BV00006B/108

9 781647 736026